LIGHT DESSERTS

ROBERT ROSE'S FAVORITE LIGHT DESSERTS

Canadian Cataloguing in Publication Data

Main entry under title:

Robert Rose's favorite light desserts

Includes index.

ISBN 1-896503-72-1

1. Desserts.   2. Low-fat diet – Recipes.   I. Title: Light desserts.

TX773.R623 1998   641.8'6   C97-932608-7

DESIGN AND PAGE COMPOSITION:	MATTHEWS COMMUNICATIONS DESIGN
PHOTOGRAPHY:	RICHARD ALLEN, MARK T. SHAPIRO (COVER)
FOOD STYLING:	ROSEMARY SUPERVILLE, SITRAM SHARMA, KATE BUSH (COVER)
RECIPE EDITOR:	LESLEIGH LANDRY

Cover photo: APPLESAUCE CARROT CAKE, PAGE 34

Distributed in the U.S. by:
Firefly Books (U.S.) Inc.
P.O. Box 1338
Ellicott Station
Buffalo, NY   14205

ORDER LINES
Tel: (416) 499-8412
Fax: (416) 499-8313

Distributed in Canada by:
Stoddart Publishing Co. Ltd.
34 Lesmill Road
North York, Ontario
M3B 2T6

ORDER LINES
Tel: (416) 445-3333
Fax: (416) 445-5967

Published by: Robert Rose Inc. • 156 Duncan Mill Road, Suite 12
Toronto, Ontario, Canada M3B 2N2   Tel: (416) 449-3535

Printed in Canada

1234567 BP 01 00 99 98

Introduction

At Robert Rose, we're committed to finding imaginative and exciting ways to provide our readers with cookbooks that offer great recipes — and exceptional value. That's the thinking behind our new "Robert Rose's Favorite" series.

Here we've selected over 50 favorite light dessert recipes from *Rose Reisman Brings Home Spa Desserts*, a book that featured over 110 low-fat, low-calorie desserts from some of North America's top spas, all adapted for home cooking. Originally published in 1991, this book is no longer widely available. So we decided to put together a special selection of these light desserts in a new format with larger type, metric equivalents for all measurements, and simple step-by-step instructions. And with full color throughout, this book is as attractive as the desserts are delicious.

All in all, it adds up to great value for anyone who loves desserts, but worries about all the fat and calories. In fact, many of the recipes we've selected for this book have less than 100 calories per serving.

So relax. Enjoy your light desserts!

Want to find out more about our books? See pages 95 and 96 for details.

Photo Prop Credits

The publisher expresses appreciation to the following suppliers of props used in the food photography appearing in this book:

B.B. BARGOON'S, TORONTO	LINENS
GRANTS FINE CHINA AND GIFTS, TORONTO	TABLEWARE
JUNORS, TORONTO	TABLEWARE
THE FLOWER CENTRE, TORONTO	FLOWERS
VILLEROY AND BOSCH LTD., TORONTO	TABLEWARE
WARES AND WARES, TORONTO	TABLEWARE

Contents

Chocolate

Cheesecake, Mousse & Soufflé

Cakes

Fruit-Based Desserts

Frozen Desserts

Pies, Tarts & Cobblers

Cookies & Breads

Chocolate

7

Serves 12

TIP

Use extra-smooth ricotta for the smoothest pastry cream.

•

Instead of putting a dollop of pastry cream on top of individual slices, carefully cut the cooled cake in half horizontally; fill cake with pastry cream and refrigerate until ready to serve.

•

Omit pastry cream and serve the cake dusted with sifted cocoa and/or sifted icing sugar and garnished with fresh raspberries.

PER SERVING

CALORIES	**226**
PROTEIN	**5 G**
FAT	**8 G**
CARBOHYDRATES	**35 G**
CHOLESTEROL	**7 MG**
SODIUM	**249 MG**

— Canyon Ranch —
ARIZONA AND MASSACHUSETTS

'Chokolate' Carob Cake with Pastry Cream

PREHEAT OVEN TO 350° F (180° C)
8-INCH (1.2 L) ROUND CAKE PAN OR 8-INCH (2 L) SPRINGFORM PAN
SPRAYED WITH BAKING SPRAY

Cake

1 cup	whole-wheat flour	250 mL
1 tsp	baking powder	5 mL
1 tsp	baking soda	5 mL
1/4 cup	canned crushed pineapple, drained	50 mL
1/2 cup	roasted carob powder, sifted	125 mL
1/3 cup	water	75 mL
1/4 cup	corn oil margarine	50 mL
3 tbsp	pineapple juice concentrate	45 mL
3/4 cup	skim milk	175 mL
1/4 cup	fructose	50 mL
2 tbsp	low-fat yogurt	25 mL
1/4 cup	sliced almonds	50 mL

Pastry Cream

1 cup	5% ricotta cheese	250 mL
1 tbsp	low-fat yogurt	15 mL
1 tbsp	fructose	15 mL
1/2 tsp	vanilla extract	2 mL

1. Make the cake: In a large bowl, stir together flour, baking powder and baking soda. Stir in pineapple and set aside.

2. In a saucepan, heat carob powder, water, margarine and pineapple juice concentrate over medium heat, stirring until carob powder dissolves and margarine melts. Cool.

3. In a food processor or blender, combine skim milk, fructose, yogurt and cooled carob mixture; purée until smooth. Stir into flour mixture just until mixed. Stir in almonds. Pour into prepared cake pan.

4. Bake 20 to 25 minutes or until tester inserted in center of cake comes out clean. Cool on wire rack.

5. Meanwhile, make the pastry cream: In a food processor or blender, combine ricotta, yogurt, fructose and vanilla; purée until smooth. Chill.

6. Serve individual slices of cake topped with a dollop of pastry cream.

Makes about 18

Chocolate Seashells

PER SERVING	
CALORIES	45
PROTEIN	1 G
FAT	1 G
CARBOHYDRATES	7 G
CHOLESTEROL	18 MG
SODIUM	64 MG

— *Golden Door* —
CALIFORNIA

PREHEAT OVEN TO 350° F (180° C)
MADELEINE COOKIE FORMS SPRAYED WITH BAKING SPRAY

2 tbsp	apple juice concentrate	25 mL
2 tbsp	honey	25 mL
1 tsp	vanilla extract	5 mL
1/4 cup	cocoa	50 mL
9 tbsp	granulated sugar *or* 7 tbsp (110 mL) fructose	140 mL
1 tbsp	butter	15 mL
1	egg	1
6 tbsp	apple juice	90 mL
2 tsp	instant coffee granules	10 mL
1/2 cup	all-purpose flour	125 mL
1/4 cup	whole-wheat flour	50 mL
1/4 cup	cocoa	50 mL
1/2 tsp	baking soda	2 mL
1/2 cup	sorbet, ice milk or frozen yogurt (optional) Icing sugar	125 mL

1. In a small saucepan, heat apple juice concentrate, honey and vanilla over medium-low heat, stirring until blended. Whisk in cocoa until smooth and thickened. Set aside to cool.

2. In a bowl cream sugar with butter; beat in egg until well mixed. Stir in cooled cocoa sauce. In a separate bowl, stir together coffee granules and apple juice until dissolved; stir into cocoa mixture. Sift together flour, whole-wheat flour, cocoa and baking soda directly onto cocoa mixture; gently fold in until well mixed. Fill cookie forms two-thirds full.

3. Bake 12 minutes or until cookies spring back when lightly touched. Cool. Dust with sifted icing sugar. If desired, slit cookie lengthwise without cutting all the way through and prop open with a small ball of sorbet.

Cocoa Kisses

TIP

It's easier to separate eggs when they're cold, but egg whites beat to a greater volume when at room temperature.

•

For extra flavor, toast the pecans in a nonstick skillet over medium-high heat, stirring occasionally, until golden and fragrant. Or, toast in a 350° F (180° C) oven for about 10 minutes.

PER SERVING (40)	
CALORIES	35
PROTEIN	1 G
FAT	1 G
CARBOHYDRATES	6 G
CHOLESTEROL	0 MG
SODIUM	8 MG

— Sonoma Mission Inn and Spa —
SAN FRANCISCO

PREHEAT OVEN TO 250° F (120° C)
BAKING SHEET SPRAYED WITH BAKING SPRAY

3	egg whites, at room temperature	3
1 cup	granulated sugar	250 mL
1/8 tsp	salt	0.5 mL
1 tsp	vanilla extract	5 mL
3 tbsp	cocoa	45 mL
1/2 cup	chopped pecans	125 mL

1. In a large bowl, beat egg whites until soft peaks form; gradually add sugar and salt, beating until mixture is glossy and stiff peaks form. Beat in vanilla. Sift cocoa into bowl; fold into meringue along with pecans.

2. Put mixture in a pastry bag fitted with star tip; pipe small kisses onto prepared baking sheet (alternatively, drop mixture by teaspoonfuls [5 mL] onto baking sheet). Bake 1 hour or until firm and dry.

Chocolate Brownies

Serves 16

PER SERVING	
CALORIES	130
PROTEIN	3 G
FAT	5 G
CARBOHYDRATES	40 G
CHOLESTEROL	20 MG
SODIUM	62 MG

King Ranch Health Spa and Fitness Resort
TORONTO

PREHEAT OVEN TO 350° F (180° C)
8-INCH (2 L) SQUARE CAKE PAN SPRAYED WITH BAKING SPRAY

6 oz	semi-sweet chocolate, chopped	175 g
1/2 cup	hot water	125 mL
4	egg whites	4
2/3 cup	granulated sugar	150 mL
1 tsp	vanilla extract	5 mL
2/3 cup	all-purpose flour	150 mL
1 tsp	baking powder	5 mL
1/8 tsp	salt	0.5 mL
	Icing sugar or low-fat yogurt (optional)	

1. In a bowl set over hot (not boiling) water, melt the chocolate with hot water, stirring until smooth; remove from heat. Beat in egg whites, sugar and vanilla until well mixed. In another bowl, stir together flour, baking powder and salt. Stir flour mixture into chocolate mixture until combined.

2. Pour batter into prepared baking dish. Bake 25 to 30 minutes or until just slightly loose at center. Cool on wire rack. If desired, dust with sifted icing sugar or, using a squeeze bottle, drizzle with yogurt.

Pots of Chocolate

TIP

Use extra-smooth ricotta for the smoothest texture.

•

Different brands of artificial sweetener may weigh and measure different amounts, but they all sweeten to the same extent. Each individual packet of artificial sweetener sweetens like 2 tsp (10 mL) sugar.

1	egg, beaten	1
1 tbsp	cold water	15 mL
1	pkg (1 tbsp [7 g]) gelatin	1
1 cup	boiling water	250 mL
1 tsp	instant coffee granules	5 mL
1/2 cup	5% ricotta cheese	125 mL
1/2 cup	skim milk	125 mL
1/4 cup	granulated sugar *or* 5 individual packets artificial sweetener	50 mL
2 1/2 tbsp	cocoa	35 mL
	Strawberries	

1. In a small bowl, stir together egg, cold water and gelatin; let stand 1 minute or until gelatin softens. Gradually add boiling water, stirring until gelatin dissolves. Transfer mixture to a food processor or blender. Add instant coffee granules, ricotta, milk, sugar and cocoa; process until smooth.

2. Divide among 6 individual dessert dishes or champagne coupes. Chill at least 2 hours. Serve garnished with strawberries.

PER SERVING

CALORIES	102
PROTEIN	5 G
FAT	3 G
CARBOHYDRATES	14 G
CHOLESTEROL	57 MG
SODIUM	49 MG

— Gurney's Inn Resort and Spa —
NEW YORK

Chocolate Angel Food Cake

PREHEAT OVEN TO 375° F (190° C)
10-INCH (4 L) TUBE PAN SPRAYED WITH BAKING SPRAY

1 cup	cake and pastry flour	250 mL
1/4 cup	cocoa	50 mL
1 1/3 cups	granulated sugar	325 mL
12	egg whites, at room temperature	12
1/2 tsp	cream of tartar	2 mL
1 tsp	vanilla extract	5 mL
1/2 tsp	almond extract	2 mL
	Strawberry purée or sliced strawberries	

1. Into a bowl, sift together flour, cocoa and 1/3 cup (75 mL) of the sugar; set aside.

2. In a large bowl, beat egg whites until foamy. Add cream of tartar; beat until soft peaks form. Gradually add remaining sugar, beating until stiff peaks form. In two additions, gently fold cocoa mixture into egg whites until well blended. Fold in vanilla and almond extracts. Pour batter into prepared pan.

3. Bake 35 to 40 minutes or until cake springs back when lightly touched. Turn pan upside down and place over a bottle or an inverted funnel. Cool cake completely before removing from pan. Serve with strawberry purée or sliced strawberries.

Cheesecake, Mousse & Soufflé

Light and Lovely Cheesecake

PREHEAT OVEN TO **350° F (180° C)**
8-INCH (2 L) SPRINGFORM PAN SPRAYED WITH BAKING SPRAY

1/4 cup	graham cracker crumbs	50 mL
3 cups	5% ricotta cheese	750 mL
1/3 cup	granulated sugar	75 mL
3	eggs	3
1/2 cup	low-fat yogurt	125 mL
1 tsp	grated lemon zest	5 mL
1 tsp	vanilla extract	5 mL
2 tbsp	cornstarch	25 mL
1 tsp	baking powder	5 mL
	Toasted sliced almonds (optional)	
1 cup	fresh raspberries (optional)	250 mL
	Raspberry purée (optional)	

1. Sprinkle graham cracker crumbs over bottom of prepared pan; set aside.

2. In a bowl or a food processor, beat ricotta with sugar until smooth. Add eggs, one at a time, beating well after each. Beat in yogurt, lemon zest and vanilla. Fold in cornstarch and baking powder until well mixed. Pour into prepared pan.

3. Bake 50 to 55 minutes or until cake is set and tester inserted in center comes out clean. Cool on wire rack. Chill. Unmold. If desired, press chopped almonds onto sides of cheesecake. Serve garnished with fresh raspberries and/or raspberry purée, if desired.

Individual Miniature Cheesecakes

PER SERVING	
CALORIES	107
PROTEIN	6 G
FAT	4 G
CARBOHYDRATES	11 G
CHOLESTEROL	43 MG
SODIUM	131 MG

— Safety Harbor Spa and Fitness Centre —
FLORIDA

PREHEAT OVEN TO 350° F (180° C)
LINE 10 MUFFIN CUPS WITH MUFFIN PAPER CUPS

1 cup	5% ricotta cheese	250 mL
1 cup	low-fat cottage cheese	250 mL
1/3 cup	granulated sugar	75 mL
1	medium egg	1
1/4 cup	light sour cream	50 mL
1/2 tsp	cornstarch	2 mL
1/8 tsp	vanilla extract	0.5 mL

Fruit purée (optional)

1. In a food processor, combine ricotta cheese, cottage cheese and sugar; purée until smooth. Beat in egg. Blend in sour cream, cornstarch and vanilla until well mixed. Divide batter among muffin cups. Set muffin tin in larger pan; pour in enough hot water to come half way up sides. Bake 30 to 35 minutes or until tester inserted in center comes out clean. Remove from water bath; cool on wire rack. Chill.

2. Serve with fruit purée, if desired.

Serves 6 to 8

Tangy Banana Cheesecake

PER SERVING (8)

CALORIES	100
PROTEIN	6 G
FAT	1 G
CARBOHYDRATES	18 G
CHOLESTEROL	3 MG
SODIUM	120 MG

— Jimmy Lesage's New Life Spa —
VERMONT

PREHEAT OVEN TO 375° F (190° C)
9-INCH (23 CM) PIE PLATE SPRAYED WITH BAKING SPRAY

1 cup	low-fat cottage cheese	250 mL
1 cup	low-fat yogurt	250 mL
2	egg whites	2
2 tbsp	lemon juice	25 mL
1 tsp	vanilla extract	5 mL
1/3 cup	whole-wheat flour	75 mL
1/4 cup	honey	50 mL
2	ripe bananas	2

Berries or sliced bananas

1. In a blender or food processor, combine cottage cheese, yogurt, egg whites, lemon juice and vanilla; purée until smooth. Add flour; blend until well mixed. With motor running, add honey through feed tube; process until smooth. Add bananas; blend until smooth. Pour into prepared pie plate.

2. Bake 30 to 40 minutes or until firm to the touch. Cool on wire rack. Chill at least 1 hour. Serve garnished with berries or sliced bananas.

Raspberry Cheesecake

Serves 12

TIP

Use fresh or frozen raspberries. If using frozen, buy individually frozen unsweetened type rather than berries packed in syrup; thaw and drain before using.

PER SERVING

CALORIES	91
PROTEIN	6 G
FAT	3 G
CARBOHYDRATES	9 G
CHOLESTEROL	57 MG
SODIUM	109 MG

— *Golden Door* —
CALIFORNIA

PREHEAT OVEN TO 350° F (180° C)
8-INCH (2 L) SPRINGFORM PAN SPRAYED WITH BAKING SPRAY

1 cup	5% ricotta cheese	250 mL
1 cup	low-fat cottage cheese	250 mL
1/3 cup	granulated sugar *or*	75 mL
	1/4 cup (50 mL) fructose	
1/3 cup	low-fat yogurt	75 mL
2	eggs	2
1 tsp	grated lemon zest	5 mL
1/2 tsp	vanilla extract	2 mL
1 tbsp	all-purpose flour	15 mL
1 1/2 tsp	cornstarch	7 mL
1 cup	raspberries	250 mL

Raspberry purée (optional)

1. In a food processor, beat together ricotta cheese, cottage cheese, sugar, yogurt, eggs, lemon zest and vanilla until smooth. Beat in flour and cornstarch. Transfer to a bowl; gently fold in raspberries. Pour into prepared pan.

2. Bake 35 minutes or until a tester inserted in center comes out clean. Cool on a wire rack. Chill. Serve plain or, if desired, with raspberry purée.

Chilled Mocha Mousse

TIP

To make carob-glazed strawberries: Melt 3 oz (75 g) carob with 1/2 tsp (2 mL) vegetable oil. With a fork or toothpick, dip half of strawberry into carob. Refrigerate on waxed paper until hardened.

PER SERVING

CALORIES	184
PROTEIN	4 G
FAT	8 G
CARBOHYDRATES	23 G
CHOLESTEROL	1 MG
SODIUM	56 MG

— **Sonoma Mission Inn and Spa** —
CALIFORNIA

6-CUP (1.5 L) SOUFFLÉ DISH OR MOLD

1/2 cup	boiling water	125 mL
2 tbsp	cocoa	25 mL
1 1/2 tbsp	instant coffee granules	22 mL
1/2 cup	cold water	125 mL
1/4 cup	cold water	50 mL
1	pkg (1 tbsp (7 g)) gelatin	1
2 tbsp	Kahlua or other coffee-flavored liqueur	25 mL
1 1/3 cups	low-fat milk powder	325 mL
2/3 cup	granulated sugar	150 mL
1/3 cup	vegetable oil	75 mL
2 tsp	lemon juice	10 mL
1 tsp	vanilla extract	5 mL

Icing sugar (optional)
Carob-dipped strawberries (optional)
(see Tip, at left)

1. In a bowl stir together boiling water, cocoa and instant coffee granules until dissolved. Stir in 1/2 cup (125 mL) cold water. Refrigerate.

2. Put 1/4 cup (50 mL) cold water in a small saucepan; sprinkle with gelatin. Let stand 1 minute. Heat gently, stirring until gelatin dissolves. Remove from heat; stir in liqueur. Stir gelatin mixture into chilled cocoa mixture until well blended. Beat in milk powder until smooth. Freeze for 15 minutes.

3. With an electric mixer on high speed, beat mixture 5 to 8 minutes or until very thick. Gradually beat in sugar. Beat in oil, lemon juice and vanilla until smooth. Pour into dish. Chill 2 hours or until set.

4. Serve dusted with sifted icing sugar or garnished with carob-dipped strawberries, if desired.

Serves 12

La Costa Cheesecake with Strawberry Sauce

TIP

Thaw unsweetened frozen strawberries for sauce or use fresh ripe berries; if using frozen, drain excess liquid before puréeing.

•

The milk powder gives an extra calcium boost to this cheesecake.

PER SERVING

CALORIES	84
PROTEIN	6 G
FAT	2 G
CARBOHYDRATES	9 G
CHOLESTEROL	53 MG
SODIUM	168 MG

— La Costa Hotel and Spa —
CALIFORNIA

PREHEAT OVEN TO **325° F (160° C)**
9-INCH (23 CM) PIE PLATE

Cheesecake

2 cups	low-fat cottage cheese	500 mL
3 tbsp	fructose	45 mL
2 tbsp	lemon juice	25 mL
2 tsp	vanilla extract	10 mL
2	eggs	2
2 tbsp	low-fat milk powder	25 mL

Strawberry Sauce

2 cups	strawberries	500 mL
1	ripe banana	1

Fresh strawberries (optional)

1. Make the cheesecake: In a blender or food processor, combine cottage cheese, fructose, lemon juice, vanilla and eggs; purée until smooth. Add milk powder; blend just until mixed. Pour into pie plate. Set pie plate in larger pan; pour in enough hot water to come half way up sides. Bake 30 to 35 minutes. Remove from water bath; cool on wire rack. Chill.

2. Make the strawberry sauce: In a blender or food processor, purée strawberries with banana until smooth.

3. To serve, drizzle 2 tbsp (25 mL) strawberry sauce over each slice of cheesecake. Garnish with strawberries, if desired.

Banana-Strawberry Mousse

Serves 6

TIP

Use fresh ripe strawberries or unsweetened frozen berries; if using frozen, thaw and drain before using.

•

For attractive orange segments, peel a whole orange with a sharp knife, removing zest, pith and membrane; cut on both sides of dividing membranes to release segments.

	PER SERVING	
CALORIES		82
PROTEIN		2 G
FAT		0.4 G
CARBOHYDRATES		19 G
CHOLESTEROL		0 MG
SODIUM		5 MG

— Gurney's Inn Resort and Spa —
MONTAUK, LONG ISLAND

3	small ripe bananas	3
1 cup	orange juice	250 mL
1 cup	strawberries	250 mL
6 tbsp	lemon juice	90 mL
1/2 cup	cold water	125 mL
1	pkg (1 tbsp [7 g]) gelatin	1

Orange segments or
sliced strawberries

1. In a blender, combine bananas, orange juice, strawberries and lemon juice; purée until smooth. Put water in a small saucepan; sprinkle with gelatin. Let stand 1 minute. Heat gently, stirring until gelatin dissolves. With motor running, pour hot gelatin through blender feed tube; purée until smooth. Divide among 6 individual dessert dishes or champagne coupes.

2. Chill 2 hours. Serve garnished with orange segments or sliced strawberries.

TIP

For a strawberry sauce, substitute strawberries for the raspberries.

•

Thaw unsweetened frozen berries for sauce or use fresh ripe berries; if using frozen, drain excess liquid before puréeing.

PER SERVING	
CALORIES	162
PROTEIN	2 G
FAT	0.3 G
CARBOHYDRATES	39 G
CHOLESTEROL	0 MG
SODIUM	35 MG

— *The Greenhouse* —
TEXAS

Fluffy Apricot Soufflé with Raspberry Sauce

PREHEAT OVEN TO 300° F (150° C)
8-CUP (2 L) SOUFFLÉ DISH SPRAYED WITH BAKING SPRAY

Soufflé

8 oz	dried apricots	250 g
1/4 cup	water	50 mL
1/4 cup	granulated sugar	50 mL
1/4 tsp	almond extract	1 mL
5	egg whites	5

Sauce

1 cup	raspberries	250 mL
Half	ripe banana	Half
1 tbsp	fruit jam (any flavor)	15 mL
1 tsp	lemon juice	5 mL

1. In a saucepan combine apricots and water; cook over medium heat 5 minutes or until all the water is absorbed. Transfer hot apricots to a food processor or blender; purée just until finely chopped. Add sugar and almond extract; purée until well mixed. Transfer to a bowl; cool mixture to room temperature.

2. In another bowl, beat egg whites until stiff peaks form. Stir one-third of egg whites into cooled apricot mixture until well mixed. Gently fold in remaining egg whites. Apricot pieces will still be evident. Pour into prepared dish.

3. Set soufflé dish in larger pan; pour in enough hot water to come half way up sides. Bake 20 minutes. Reduce oven temperature to 250° F (120° C); bake 12 minutes longer or until light brown and no longer loose. Meanwhile, make the raspberry sauce: In a blender or food processor, combine raspberries, banana, jam and lemon juice; purée until smooth. Strain to remove seeds.

4. Serve soufflé hot, drizzled with raspberry sauce.

Cakes

Cinnamon Date Coffee Cake

PREHEAT OVEN TO 350° F (180° C)
8-CUP (2 L) BUNDT PAN SPRAYED WITH BAKING SPRAY

3/4 cup	granulated sugar	175 mL
3 tbsp	softened butter	45 mL
2	egg whites	2
1	egg	1
1 1/3 cups	low-fat yogurt	325 mL
3 tbsp	lemon juice	45 mL
1 tsp	vanilla extract	5 mL
2 cups	all-purpose flour	500 mL
1 tsp	baking powder	5 mL
1 tsp	baking soda	5 mL
1 tsp	cinnamon	5 mL
1/8 tsp	nutmeg	0.5 mL
2/3 cup	chopped dates	150 mL
1/4 cup	packed brown sugar	50 mL

Icing sugar
Extra sliced dates (optional)

1. In a bowl, beat together sugar, butter, egg whites and egg until smooth. Beat in yogurt, lemon juice and vanilla. In another bowl, sift together flour, baking powder, baking soda, cinnamon and nutmeg; stir into yogurt mixture just until combined.

2. In a small bowl, stir together brown sugar and dates. Pour half of cake batter into prepared pan and sprinkle with half of date mixture. Repeat. Bake 40 minutes or until tester inserted in center comes out clean. Cool in pan for 5 minutes; invert and cool completely on wire rack. Serve dusted with sifted icing sugar and garnished with sliced dates, if desired.

Serves 6

Strawberry Shortcake

TIP

Instead of making shortcakes, use 2 large lady fingers per serving. Or, use 12 oz (375 g) store-bought sponge cake; divide into 6 pieces, then cut each piece in half to form a sandwich.

PER SERVING

CALORIES	149
PROTEIN	4 G
FAT	2 G
CARBOHYDRATES	26 G
CHOLESTEROL	80 MG
SODIUM	39 MG

— Palm-Aire —
POMPANO BEACH, FLORIDA

PREHEAT OVEN TO 350° F (180° C)
6-CUP MUFFIN TIN SPRAYED WITH BAKING SPRAY

Shortcakes

2	eggs	2
3/4 cup	granulated sugar *or* 1/2 cup (125 mL) fructose	175 mL
1/4 tsp	vanilla extract	1 mL
1/8 tsp	ground cardamom (optional)	0.5 mL
Pinch	nutmeg	Pinch
1/3 cup	all-purpose flour	75 mL

Toppings

6 oz	dessert topping mix	175 g
1 cup	ice water	250 mL
2 cups	halved fresh strawberries	500 mL

Mint leaves

1. Make shortcakes: In a bowl, beat eggs with sugar for 5 minutes or until thickened and creamy. Beat in vanilla, cardamom (if desired) and nutmeg. Fold in flour until well mixed. Divide batter among muffin cups. Bake for 10 to 12 minutes or until golden and tester inserted in center comes out clean. Remove from muffin tins; cool on wire rack.

2. Split cooled shortcakes in half horizontally; place bottom halves on six individual dessert dishes. Beat dessert topping mix with ice water until soft peaks form. Spoon some dessert topping onto each shortcake bottom, top each with a few strawberries and replace shortcake tops. Divide remaining dessert topping and strawberries among shortcakes. Serve garnished with mint leaves.

TIP

Eggs separate more easily when cold. Use 3 bowls — one to separate eggs over, one for the yolks and one to hold the perfectly clean whites. Make sure there's not a speck of yolk in the whites or they won't beat properly.

PER SERVING	
CALORIES	143
PROTEIN	5 G
FAT	2 G
CARBOHYDRATES	26 G
CHOLESTEROL	90 MG
SODIUM	56 MG

— Gurney's Inn Resort and Spa —
MONTAUK, LONG ISLAND

Chiffon Cake

PREHEAT OVEN TO 350° F (180° C)
9-INCH (2.5 L) SPRINGFORM PAN SPRAYED WITH BAKING SPRAY

1 cup	cake and pastry flour	250 mL
1/2 cup	granulated sugar	125 mL
1 1/2 tsp	baking powder	7 mL
3	medium eggs	3
2	medium egg whites	2
1/3 cup	water	75 mL
1 tsp	grated lemon zest	5 mL
1 tsp	grated orange zest	5 mL
1/2 tsp	vanilla extract	2 mL
1/2 cup	egg whites (about 4 medium egg whites)	125 mL
1/4 tsp	cream of tartar	1 mL

Sliced fresh fruit

1. Sift flour, sugar and baking powder into a bowl. In another bowl, beat together whole eggs, 2 egg whites, water, lemon zest, orange zest and vanilla until well mixed. Slowly add wet ingredients to dry ingredients, mixing until combined. Set aside.

2. In a separate bowl, beat egg whites until foamy. Add cream of tartar; beat until stiff peaks form. Gently fold egg whites into batter. Pour into prepared pan. Bake 25 to 30 minutes or until tester inserted in center comes out clean. Cool on wire rack.

3. Serve garnished with sliced fresh fruit.

Orange Coffee Cake

Serves 10 to 12

PER SERVING (12)	
CALORIES	136
PROTEIN	3 G
FAT	3 G
CARBOHYDRATES	24 G
CHOLESTEROL	51 MG
SODIUM	225 MG

— Doral Saturnia —
FLORIDA

PREHEAT OVEN TO 350° F (180° C)
8-CUP (2 L) BUNDT PAN SPRAYED WITH BAKING SPRAY

2 cups	orange juice	500 mL
2 tsp	grated orange zest	10 mL
1 cup	granulated sugar	250 mL
1/4 cup	butter	50 mL
3	medium eggs	3
1 cup	all-purpose flour	250 mL
1 cup	whole-wheat flour	250 mL
2 tsp	baking soda	10 mL

Icing sugar
Sliced fresh strawberries

1. In a saucepan combine orange juice and orange zest; bring to a boil. Remove from heat, transfer to a bowl and refrigerate until cool.

2. In a bowl, cream sugar with butter; add eggs, one at a time, beating well after each. In another bowl, stir together flour, whole-wheat flour and baking soda. Add to creamed mixture alternately with orange juice, making three additions of flour and two of orange juice. Pour into prepared pan. Bake 35 to 40 minutes or until tester inserted in center comes out clean. Cool in pan for 5 minutes; invert and cool completely on wire rack.

3. Serve dusted with sifted icing sugar and garnished with sliced strawberries.

Serves 32

PER SERVING	
CALORIES	75
PROTEIN	2 G
FAT	2 G
CARBOHYDRATES	28 G
CHOLESTEROL	11 MG
SODIUM	90 MG

— *The Heartland* —
ILLINOIS

Applesauce Carrot Cake

PREHEAT OVEN TO 350° F (180° C)
8-CUP (2 L) BUNDT PAN SPRAYED WITH BAKING SPRAY

2 1/3 cups	whole-wheat flour	575 mL
4 tsp	cinnamon	20 mL
2 tsp	baking powder	10 mL
1 tsp	baking soda	5 mL
1/2 tsp	nutmeg	2 mL
1/4 tsp	allspice	1 mL
1/4 tsp	salt	1 mL
1 cup	unsweetened applesauce	250 mL
3/4 cup	honey	175 mL
1/3 cup	corn oil	75 mL
3	eggs	3
2 cups	grated carrots	500 mL

Lemon cream frosting (optional)
(see recipe, page 37)
Lemon, orange and/or lime zest
cut into thin strips (optional)

1. In a large bowl, stir together flour, cinnamon, baking powder, baking soda, nutmeg, allspice and salt. In another bowl, beat together applesauce, honey, oil and eggs; gradually stir into flour mixture until well mixed. Stir in grated carrots. Pour into prepared pan.

2. Bake 35 minutes or until tester inserted in center comes out clean. Cool in pan for 5 minutes; invert and cool completely on wire rack. Ice with lemon cream frosting and garnish with zest, if desired. Store in refrigerator.

Banana Cake with Lemon Cream Frosting

PREHEAT OVEN TO 350° F (180° C)
13- BY 9-INCH (3.5 L) CAKE PAN SPRAYED WITH BAKING SPRAY

Cake

1 3/4 cups	whole-wheat flour	425 mL
2 tsp	baking powder	10 mL
3/4 tsp	baking soda	4 mL
1/2 cup	buttermilk	125 mL
1/2 cup	honey	125 mL
1/4 cup	walnut oil *or* vegetable oil	50 mL
3	ripe bananas	3
4	egg whites	4

Lemon Cream Frosting

1 cup	5% ricotta cheese	250 mL
1 1/2 tbsp	honey	22 mL
1 tbsp	grated lemon zest	15 mL
1 tbsp	lemon juice	15 mL
1 1/2 tsp	cornstarch *or* arrowroot	7 mL
1/4 cup	chopped walnuts	50 mL
	Lemon zest cut into thin strips	

1. Make the cake: In a bowl stir together flour, baking powder and baking soda; set aside. In a food processor or blender, purée buttermilk, honey, oil and bananas until smooth; stir into flour mixture just until mixed. In another bowl, beat egg whites until stiff peaks form; fold into batter. Pour into prepared pan. Bake 20 to 30 minutes or until tester inserted in center comes out clean. Cool in pan on wire rack.

2. Make the frosting: In a food processor, purée ricotta, honey, lemon zest, lemon juice and cornstarch until smooth. Transfer to a saucepan. Cook over medium heat, stirring constantly, until steaming hot. Remove from heat. Chill.

3. Spread cold frosting over cooled cake. Sprinkle with walnuts and strips of lemon zest.

Blueberry Honey Cake

PREHEAT OVEN TO 350° F (180° C)
9-INCH (1.5 L) ROUND CAKE PAN SPRAYED WITH BAKING SPRAY

1 cup	fresh or frozen blueberries	250 mL
1/3 cup	honey	75 mL
1/3 cup	water	75 mL
1 tbsp	cornstarch *or* arrowroot	15 mL
1 tbsp	water	15 mL
1 1/2 cups	whole-wheat flour	375 mL
1 tsp	baking powder	5 mL
1 cup	2% milk	250 mL
1/3 cup	honey	75 mL
1 tbsp	vegetable oil	15 mL

1. In a saucepan combine blueberries, honey and 1/3 cup (75 mL) water; bring to a boil over medium heat. Stir together cornstarch and 1 tbsp (15 mL) water; add to simmering blueberry mixture. Cook, stirring constantly, until thickened. Remove from heat; set aside.

2. In a large bowl, stir together flour and baking powder. In another bowl, whisk together milk, honey and oil until smooth; add to flour mixture, stirring to combine. Pour into prepared pan. Pour blueberry mixture on top of batter. Bake 25 to 35 minutes or until tester inserted in center comes out clean.

— *Canyon Ranch* —
ARIZONA AND MASSACHUSETTS

Serves 8

TIP

For extra walnut flavor, toast the walnuts before chopping. Toast nuts in a nonstick skillet over medium-high heat, stirring occasionally, until golden and fragrant. Or, toast in a 350° F (180° C) oven for about 10 minutes.

PER SERVING

CALORIES	90
PROTEIN	3 G
FAT	3 G
CARBOHYDRATES	12 G
CHOLESTEROL	34 MG
SODIUM	164 MG

Carrot Buttermilk Cake

PREHEAT OVEN TO 325° F (160° C)
8-INCH (2 L) SPRINGFORM PAN OR 8-INCH (2 L) SQUARE CAKE PAN
SPRAYED WITH BAKING SPRAY

Cake

1/2 cup	whole wheat flour	125 mL
1/2 tsp	baking soda	2 mL
1/2 tsp	cinnamon	2 mL
1	egg yolk	1
4 tsp	buttermilk	20 mL
4 tsp	fructose	20 mL
1 tbsp	corn oil	15 mL
1/2 tsp	vanilla extract	2 mL
1/2 cup	grated carrots	125 mL
1/4 cup	drained crushed pineapple	50 mL
2 tsp	chopped walnuts	10 mL
2	egg whites	2

Glaze

2 tbsp	buttermilk	25 mL
4 tsp	fructose	20 mL
1/2 tsp	corn syrup	2 mL
1/2 tsp	corn oil margarine	2 mL
Pinch	baking soda	Pinch
1/2 tsp	vanilla extract	2 mL

1. Make the cake: Sift flour, baking soda and cinnamon into a large bowl. In another bowl, whisk together egg yolk, buttermilk, fructose, corn oil and vanilla; add to flour mixture and stir until combined. Stir in carrots, pineapple and walnuts.

2. In a separate bowl, beat egg whites until stiff peaks form. Gently fold into batter until well mixed. Pour into prepared pan. Bake 25 to 30 minutes or until center springs back when lightly touched. Cool slightly on wire rack while making glaze.

Recipe continues next page...

3. Make the glaze: In a small saucepan combine butter-milk, fructose, corn syrup, margarine and baking soda. Bring to a boil; reduce heat to low and cook for 5 minutes. Remove from heat. Stir in vanilla.

4. With a fork, poke holes in top of warm cake; pour hot glaze over cake. Serve warm or at room temperature.

Fruit-Based Desserts

Serves 10 to 12

TIP

Make the crêpes ahead of time — stack with pieces of waxed paper between crêpes, wrap well and store in refrigerator for up to 3 days or in freezer for up to 2 months.

•

Don't be discouraged if your first crêpe isn't perfectly round — with practice, the crêpes' appearance will improve.

PER SERVING (12)	
CALORIES	96
PROTEIN	3 G
FAT	1 G
CARBOHYDRATES	40 G
CHOLESTEROL	40 MG
SODIUM	90 MG

— Canyon Ranch —
ARIZONA AND MASSACHUSETTS

Fruit Blintzes

PREHEAT OVEN TO 350° F (180° C)
BAKING SHEET

Crêpes

1 cup	skim milk	250 mL
3/4 cup	whole-wheat flour	175 mL
1	egg	1
1/8 tsp	salt	0.5 mL

Filling

2 cups	5% ricotta cheese	500 mL
2 tbsp	granulated sugar *or* 4 tsp (20 mL)fructose	25 mL
2 tsp	lemon juice	10 mL
2 tsp	vanilla extract	10 mL
1/2 tsp	cinnamon	2 mL
1 cup	fresh berries and/or sliced fresh fruit	250 mL
1/4 cup	raisins	50 mL

Sauce (optional)

1 cup	low-fat yogurt	250 mL
2 tbsp	apple juice concentrate	25 mL
1 tsp	vanilla extract	5 mL

Icing sugar
Grated lemon and/or orange zest

1. Make the crêpes: In a blender, combine milk, flour, egg and salt; purée until smooth. Spray an 8-inch (20 cm) nonstick frying pan with baking spray; heat over medium-high heat. Pour 2 tbsp (25 mL) crêpe batter into pan, tilting pan from side to side to distribute batter evenly. Cook until edges curl away from sides of pan and underside is golden; turn and cook until other side is golden. Remove from pan. Repeat with remaining crêpe batter, respraying the pan with baking spray as necessary. You will get 10 to 12 crêpes.

2. Make the filling: In a food processor, combine ricotta cheese, sugar, lemon juice, vanilla and cinnamon; blend until smooth. Stir in fruit and raisins. Divide mixture evenly among crêpes, placing filling on bottom third of crepe. Roll crêpes up and transfer to baking sheet. Bake for 8 minutes. Meanwhile, make the sauce (if desired).

3. Sauce: In a bowl, stir together yogurt, apple juice concentrate and vanilla until well mixed.

4. Serve blintzes warm, dusted with sifted icing sugar and garnished with grated citrus zest. Serve with some sauce spooned over each blintz.

Serves 4

TIP

Use fresh or frozen raspberries to make purée. If using frozen, buy unsweetened variety; thaw and drain before puréeing.

•

If you prefer, use dessert topping mix made with water instead of egg white and fructose topping.

•

Straining the purée removes raspberry seeds.

Peach Melba

2	ripe peaches	2
1/2 cup	strained raspberry purée	125 mL
1 tbsp	fruit juice concentrate (apple or orange)	15 mL
1	egg white	1
1 tbsp	fructose	15 mL
4	fresh raspberries	4

1. Peel peaches; cut in half, removing pits. Place a peach half in each of 4 individual dessert bowls. In a bowl, stir together raspberry purée and fruit juice concentrate. Pour over peaches, dividing evenly.

2. In a bowl, beat egg white until soft peaks form. Gradually add fructose, beating until stiff peaks form. Spoon over peaches. Garnish each with a fresh raspberry.

PER SERVING	
CALORIES	52
PROTEIN	1 G
FAT	0.1 G
CARBOHYDRATES	12 G
CHOLESTEROL	0 MG
SODIUM	14 MG

La Costa Hotel and Spa
CALIFORNIA

Serves 8

Key Lime Dessert

PREHEAT OVEN TO 400° F (200° C)
4-CUP (1 L) SOUFFLÉ DISH OR EIGHT 1/2-CUP (125 mL) RAMEKINS

TIP

To get the most juice from limes or other citrus fruit, bring fruit to room temperature before juicing.

•

Eggs are most easily separated cold, straight from the refrigerator.

•

Make sure the egg whites for the meringue are perfectly pure, without a speck of yolk, or they will not beat properly. Egg whites beat to a greater volume if at room temperature.

Filling

3/4 cup	fructose	175 mL
1/4 cup	cornstarch	50 mL
1 1/2 cups	water	375 mL
2	egg whites, at room temperature	2
1	egg, at room temperature	1
2 tsp	grated lime zest	10 mL
1/4 cup	freshly squeezed lime juice	50 mL

Meringue

2	egg whites	2
1/4 tsp	cream of tartar	1 mL
4 tsp	fructose	20 mL

PER SERVING

CALORIES	120
PROTEIN	3 G
FAT	1 G
CARBOHYDRATES	25 G
CHOLESTEROL	37 MG
SODIUM	43 MG

— Canyon Ranch —
ARIZONA AND MASSACHUSETTS

1. Make the filling: In a saucepan, stir together fructose and cornstarch. Gradually whisk in water until smooth. Bring to a boil over medium heat, stirring constantly. Continue to boil for 1 minute, stirring constantly, or until thickened. Remove from heat.

2. In a bowl beat egg whites with egg. Gradually whisk half of hot cornstarch mixture into egg mixture. Pour back into remaining cornstarch mixture. Return saucepan to medium heat; cook, stirring, 1 minute. Remove from heat. Stir in lime zest and juice. Pour into soufflé dish.

3. Make the meringue: In a bowl, beat egg whites until foamy. Add cream of tartar and beat until soft peaks form. Gradually add fructose, beating until stiff peaks form. Spoon over hot filling. Bake 8 to 10 minutes or until golden brown.

Melon Balls with Warm Ginger Sauce

1	small ripe honeydew melon	1
2	small ripe cantaloupes	2

Sauce

2 cups	orange juice	500 mL
2 tbsp	minced ginger root *or* 1/2 tsp (2 mL) ground ginger	25 mL
1 tbsp	raspberry or red wine vinegar	15 mL
1 tsp	honey	5 mL
1/2 tsp	lemon juice	2 mL

Fresh mint leaves

1. Cut melons in half and discard seeds. With a melon baller, scoop out flesh. Divide melon balls among 6 individual dessert dishes.

2. In a saucepan combine orange juice, ginger, vinegar, honey and lemon juice. Bring to a boil; cook until reduced to 1/2 cup (125 mL). Spoon warm sauce over melon balls and serve garnished with mint leaves.

Blueberry Apple Crisp

PREHEAT OVEN TO 350° F (180° C)
9-INCH (2.5 L) SQUARE BAKING DISH

3	medium apples, peeled, cored and sliced	3
1 cup	fresh blueberries	250 mL
1/4 cup	apple juice	50 mL
2 tbsp	granulated sugar	25 mL
1 tbsp	lemon juice	15 mL
1 tsp	cinnamon	5 mL

PER SERVING	
CALORIES	115
PROTEIN	1 G
FAT	2 G
CARBOHYDRATES	23 G
CHOLESTEROL	5 MG
SODIUM	20 MG

— Doral Saturnia —
FLORIDA

Topping

1 cup	rolled oats	250 mL
1/3 cup	whole wheat flour	75 mL
1/4 cup	packed brown sugar	50 mL
2 tbsp	apple juice	25 mL
2 tbsp	softened butter	25 mL
1/2 tsp	cinnamon	2 mL

1. In a bowl, mix together apples, blueberries, apple juice, sugar, lemon juice and cinnamon. Transfer to baking dish.

2. Make topping: In a bowl, stir together rolled oats, flour, brown sugar, apple juice, butter and cinnamon until crumbly. Sprinkle over blueberry mixture.

3. Bake 30 minutes or until golden. Serve warm or cold.

Serves 6

TIP

Use a firm pear such as a Bosc.

PER SERVING	
CALORIES	167
PROTEIN	1 G
FAT	3 G
CARBOHYDRATES	37 G
CHOLESTEROL	0 MG
SODIUM	7 MG

— The Pointe —
ARIZONA

Poached Pears in Chocolate Sauce

2 tbsp	lemon juice	25 mL
6	small ripe pears	6
1 1/2 cups	pear nectar (or other fruit nectar)	375 mL
1/4 cup	semi-sweet chocolate chips	50 mL
1 tbsp	2% evaporated milk	15 mL

1. Put lemon juice and 6 cups (1.5 L) water in a bowl. Peel pears, leaving whole with stems intact and dropping each in water mixture as it is peeled. Drain. In a saucepan, combine pears and pear nectar. Bring to a boil, reduce heat to medium-low, cover and cook, turning pears over halfway through, for 20 to 25 minutes or until tender when pierced with a knife. Transfer pears and syrup to a bowl; chill.

2. Before serving, drain pears, reserving syrup. Bring syrup to a boil; cook until reduced to 1/4 cup (50 mL). Stir in chocolate chips until melted. Beat in evaporated milk until smooth.

3. Serve chilled pears on top of a pool of hot chocolate sauce.

Apple Strudel with Cinnamon Sauce

PREHEAT OVEN TO 400° F (200° C)
BAKING SHEET

1 1/4 lbs	apples (about 4)	625 g
1 tbsp	fructose	15 mL
1/2 tsp	cinnamon	2 mL
1/4 tsp	nutmeg	1 mL
1/4 cup	raisins (optional)	50 mL
4	sheets phyllo pastry	4

Cinnamon Sauce (optional)

2 tsp	cornstarch *or* arrowroot	10 mL
1 tbsp	water	15 mL
1 cup	apple cider	250 mL

Icing sugar

1. Peel, core and slice apples. In a bowl toss apple slices with fructose, cinnamon, nutmeg and, if desired, raisins.

2. Layer phyllo sheets one on top of the other. Put apple filling on phyllo, along short end. Roll up carefully. Tuck ends under; transfer to baking sheet. Bake 25 to 30 minutes or until golden. Meanwhile, make the sauce, if desired.

3. Cinnamon sauce: Dissolve cornstarch in water. In a small saucepan, bring apple cider to a boil; whisk in dissolved cornstarch. Cook, whisking, until sauce thickens.

4. Dust strudel with sifted icing sugar; serve sliced strudel with warm sauce.

— Cal-A-Vie —
CALIFORNIA

Serves 5

TIP

Make the sabayon up to 2 days ahead; store, covered, in the refrigerator.

•

If you don't have orange liqueur, use whatever liqueur you have on hand.

•

Use any combination of fresh fruit and berries.

PER SERVING

CALORIES	157
PROTEIN	4 G
FAT	7 G
CARBOHYDRATES	20 G
CHOLESTEROL	163 MG
SODIUM	9 MG

Fruit Mosaic with Sabayon Sauce

5 INDIVIDUAL OVENPROOF DESSERT DISHES

Sabayon

3	egg yolks	3
1/2 cup	white wine	125 mL
2 tbsp	sweet white wine	25 mL
1 tbsp	orange flavored liqueur	15 mL
1 tsp	grated lemon zest	5 mL
2 tsp	granulated sugar (optional)	10 mL

Fruit

1 cup	fresh raspberries	250 mL
5	strawberries	5
2	kiwi fruit, peeled and sliced	2
2	oranges, divided into segments	2
1/4 cup	ground almonds	50 mL

1. In a bowl set over a pot of simmering water, whisk together egg yolks, white wine, sweet wine, liqueur and lemon zest. Cook, whisking, 3 minutes or until smooth and thickened (do not boil). Remove from heat. If desired, whisk in sugar until smooth. Cool to room temperature.

2. Preheat broiler. Spread sabayon over bottom of dessert dishes. Arrange fruit in a colorful pattern over sabayon. Sprinkle ground almonds over fruit. Broil 2 to 3 minutes or until nuts are golden. Serve immediately.

Frozen Desserts

Serves 20

TIP

Omit strawberry purée and serve with 1 cup (250 mL) of sliced strawberries instead.

PER SERVING	
CALORIES	135
PROTEIN	3 G
FAT	4 G
CARBOHYDRATES	20 G
CHOLESTEROL	87 MG
SODIUM	43 MG

Rancho La Puerta
MEXICO

Frozen Lemon Roulade

PREHEAT OVEN TO 375° F (190° C)
15- BY 10-INCH (40 BY 25 CM) JELLY ROLL PAN, LINED WITH
PARCHMENT PAPER AND SPRAYED WITH BAKING SPRAY

Genoise Cake

5	eggs	5
1/2 cup	fructose	125 mL
1 1/4 tsp	nutmeg	6 mL
1 tsp	grated lemon zest	5 mL
1 tsp	vanilla extract	5 mL
3/4 cup	all-purpose flour	175 mL
	Icing sugar	

Lemon Ice Milk

4 cups	vanilla ice milk *or* frozen vanilla yogurt, softened	1 L
2 tbsp	grated lemon zest	25 mL
1/2 cup	lemon juice	125 mL
1 tsp	lemon extract (optional)	5 mL
1/2 cup	strawberry purée	125 mL
	Extra grated lemon zest	

1. Make the genoise: Beat eggs with fructose until thick and creamy. Stir in nutmeg, lemon zest and vanilla. Fold in flour. Pour into prepared jelly roll pan, spreading to edges. Bake for 12 to 15 minutes or until puffy and golden. Let cool 5 minutes. Invert onto a clean tea towel dusted with sifted icing sugar. Dust with more sifted icing sugar. Remove jelly roll pan and carefully peel paper away from cake. Starting at the short end, roll cake and tea towel up together. Cool completely.

2. Make the lemon ice milk: In a bowl, beat ice milk, lemon zest, lemon juice and, if desired, lemon extract until well combined. Unroll cake and tea towel. Spread lemon ice milk evenly over genoise. Roll cake up. Wrap in plastic wrap. Freeze until firm.

3. Dust roulade with sifted icing sugar. Cut cake into 1/2-inch (1 cm) slices. Serve on top of a pool of strawberry purée and garnish with lemon zest.

Serves 6

Honey Vanilla Ice Cream with Hot Spiced Apples

TIP

Don't worry if you don't have an ice cream maker. Pour chilled ice cream mixture into a loaf pan lined with plastic wrap and freeze until solid. Transfer to a food processor; pulse on and off until smooth. Store in freezer until ready to serve.

PER SERVING	
CALORIES	186
PROTEIN	6 G
FAT	6 G
CARBOHYDRATES	27 G
CHOLESTEROL	276 MG
SODIUM	41 MG

— Four Seasons Resort and Club —
TEXAS

Ice Cream

2 cups	2% milk	500 mL
3 tbsp	honey	45 mL
1/8 tsp	vanilla extract	0.5 mL
6	egg yolks	6

Spiced Apple Mixture

3	apples	3
2 cups	apple juice	500 mL
1/4 tsp	cinnamon	1 mL
1/8 tsp	ground ginger	0.5 mL
1/8 tsp	nutmeg	0.5 mL
2 tbsp	cornstarch	25 mL
1 tbsp	water	15 mL

1. Make the ice cream: In a saucepan bring milk, honey and vanilla to a boil; reduce heat to low. In a bowl, beat egg yolks. Whisk a little of the hot milk into yolk mixture, then pour back into remaining milk. Whisk constantly over low heat until mixture is thick enough to coat a spoon; do not boil. Remove from heat. Chill. In an ice cream maker, freeze according to manufacturer's directions.

2. Make the spiced apple mixture: Peel, core and thinly slice the apples. Put in a saucepan along with apple juice, cinnamon, ginger and nutmeg. Bring to a boil, reduce heat and simmer 5 minutes. Dissolve cornstarch in water; stir into simmering apple mixture and cook 1 minute longer or until thickened. Remove from heat. Cool slightly. Serve over ice cream.

Baked Alaska

TIP

Use any flavors of ice milk you like.

PER SERVING

CALORIES	254
PROTEIN	6 G
FAT	9 G
CARBOHYDRATES	35 G
CHOLESTEROL	35 MG
SODIUM	136 MG

— *Palm-Aire* —
FLORIDA

8- OR 9-INCH (2 OR 2.5 L) SPRINGFORM PAN
BAKING SHEET

12 oz	store-bought sponge cake	375 g
2 cups	chocolate ice milk, softened	500 mL
2 cups	strawberry ice milk, softened	500 mL
2 cups	vanilla ice milk, softened	500 mL

Meringue

4	egg whites	4
1/3 cup	granulated sugar	75 mL

1. Cut sponge cake into 1/4-inch (0.5 cm) slices. Line bottom and sides of springform pan with slices, cutting them to fit and saving enough for the top.

2. Spoon chocolate ice milk over sponge cake. Top with strawberry ice milk, then vanilla ice milk. Top with sliced sponge cake to completely enclose ice milk. Freeze 1 1/2 hours or until solid.

3. Preheat oven to 450° F (220° C). Beat egg whites until soft peaks form. Gradually add sugar, beating until stiff peaks form. Put springform pan on baking sheet; remove sides of springform pan. Spoon meringue over top and sides of cake. Bake 5 to 10 minutes or until golden. Serve immediately. Store any leftovers in freezer.

Serves 6

TIP

Don't worry if you don't have an ice cream maker. Pour raspberry mixture into a loaf pan lined with plastic wrap and freeze until solid. Transfer to a food processor; pulse on and off until smooth. Store in freezer until ready to serve.

PER SERVING

CALORIES	60
PROTEIN	1 G
FAT	0.4 G
CARBOHYDRATES	14 G
CHOLESTEROL	1 MG
SODIUM	10 MG

— Maine Chance Fitness and Beauty Resort —
ARIZONA

Raspberry Ice with Fresh Strawberries

4 1/2 cups	fresh raspberries	1.125 L
	Honey to taste	
6 tbsp	low-fat yogurt (optional)	90 mL
6	large fresh strawberries	6
	Fresh mint leaves	

1. In a blender or food processor, purée raspberries. Strain to remove seeds. Stir in honey to taste. In an ice cream maker, freeze according to manufacturer's directions.

2. Divide among 6 individual dessert dishes. Spoon 1 tbsp (15 mL) yogurt on top of each serving, if desired. Garnish each serving with a strawberry and mint leaves.

Pineapple Lime Sorbet

TIP

If don't have an ice cream maker, pour into a baking dish and freeze until solid. Break into small pieces; in a food processor, pulse on and off until smooth. Store in freezer until ready to serve.

•

Purée canned crushed pineapple for the smoothest texture.

PER SERVING

CALORIES	56
PROTEIN	1 G
FAT	0.2 G
CARBOHYDRATES	15 G
CHOLESTEROL	0 MG
SODIUM	10 MG

— Norwich Inn and Spa —
CONNECTICUT

1 1/4 cups	pineapple purée	300 mL
2 tsp	grated lime or lemon zest	10 mL
3/4 cup	freshly squeezed lime or lemon juice	175 mL
1/4 cup	water	50 mL
	Granulated sugar to taste (optional)	
	Thin slices lime or lemon	

1. In a bowl, stir together pineapple purée, lime zest and juice, water and, if desired, sugar.

2. In an ice cream maker, freeze according to manufacturer's directions.

3. . Divide among 4 individual dessert dishes. Serve garnished with thin slices of lime.

Frozen Jamoca Mousse

Serves 12

1 cup	5% ricotta cheese	250 mL
2 cups	low-fat yogurt	500 mL
1/2 cup	fructose	125 mL
4 tsp	cocoa	20 mL
2 tsp	instant coffee granules	10 mL
1 tsp	vanilla extract	5 mL

1. In a food processor or blender, purée ricotta, yogurt, fructose, cocoa, coffee granules and vanilla until smooth.

2. In an ice cream maker, freeze according to manufacturer's directions.

PER SERVING	
CALORIES	77
PROTEIN	3 G
FAT	2 G
CARBOHYDRATES	11 G
CHOLESTEROL	7 MG
SODIUM	39 MG

— The Heartland —
ILLINOIS

Tulip Cookies with Fruit Sorbet

TIP

Use your favorite flavor of sorbet, or use ice milk.

•

To save time, make the tulip cups assembly-line fashion. Use 2 baking sheets; while one tray bakes, spread the batter on the next tray, then put it in the oven just as you remove the last batch.

•

The cookies must be shaped while they are warm, so work quickly. If cookie cools and is too firm to shape, return to oven for 30 seconds or until softened.

PREHEAT OVEN TO 350° F (180° C)
BAKING SHEET SPRAYED WITH BAKING SPRAY

3/4 cup	buttermilk	175 mL
1	egg	1
6 tbsp	granulated sugar	90 mL
1/3 cup	whole-wheat flour	75 mL
1/3 cup	all-purpose flour	75 mL
1/8 tsp	cinnamon	0.5 mL
1/8 tsp	salt	0.5 mL

Raspberry or mango sorbet
Fresh raspberries
or sliced ripe mango

1. In a bowl stir together buttermilk, egg, sugar, whole-wheat flour, flour, cinnamon and salt until smooth. Let batter rest for 20 minutes.

2. Place 1 tbsp (15 mL) batter at one end of prepared baking sheet. With the back of a spoon, spread to form a circle 5 inches (12 cm) in diameter. Repeat with another 1 tbsp (15 mL) batter on other half of baking sheet. Bake for 9 to 11 minutes or until golden. With a spatula, remove hot cookies from baking sheet and place each over bottom of a glass, pressing gently to create fluted effect. Cool completely on glass.

3. Repeat with remaining batter, respraying baking sheet between batches.

4. Serve each tulip cup with a small scoop of sorbet, garnished with fresh fruit.

PHOTOGRAPH ON FACING PAGE.

PER SERVING

CALORIES	60
PROTEIN	2 G
FAT	0.4 G
CARBOHYDRATES	13 G
CHOLESTEROL	12 MG
SODIUM	37 MG

— Doral Saturnia —
FLORIDA

Frozen Orange Cream

1 tbsp	grated orange zest	15 mL
1 1/3 cups	orange juice	325 mL
2/3 cup	skim milk	150 mL

1. In a food processor or blender, purée orange zest, orange juice and milk.
2. In an ice cream maker, freeze according to manufacturer's directions.

Pies, Tarts & Cobblers

Lemon Meringue Pie

TIP

For a more traditional look, use a 9-inch (23 cm) pie plate.

•

Use lime juice and zest instead of lemon.

•

Separate eggs carefully for meringue — egg whites contaminated with yolk will not beat properly. Also, make sure your bowls and beaters are perfectly clean when making meringue.

PER SERVING

CALORIES	110
PROTEIN	1 G
FAT	1 G
CARBOHYDRATES	25 G
CHOLESTEROL	0 MG
SODIUM	26 MG

— Four Seasons Resort and Club —
TEXAS

PREHEAT OVEN TO 450° F (220° C)
SIX 1/2-CUP (125 mL) OVENPROOF DISHES
BAKING SHEET

Filling

1 1/4 cups	water	300 mL
1/2 cup	fructose	125 mL
1 tsp	grated lemon zest	5 mL
1/4 cup	lemon juice	50 mL
1/4 cup	cornstarch	50 mL
3/4 cup	water	175 mL
1 tsp	margarine	5 mL

Meringue

2	egg whites	2
1 tbsp	fructose	15 mL

1. Make pie filling: In a saucepan combine 1 1/4 cups (300 mL) water, fructose, lemon zest and juice. Bring to a boil. In a bowl, stir together cornstarch and 3/4 cup (175 mL) water until dissolved. Stir into boiling lemon mixture. Cook, stirring, until thickened. Remove from heat. Stir in margarine. Divide among dishes. Cool.

2. Make the meringue: In a bowl, beat egg whites until soft peaks form. Gradually add fructose, beating until stiff peaks form. Spoon over filling; transfer dishes to baking sheet. Bake 5 minutes or until golden. Cool to room temperature. Chill before serving.

Serves 8

Strawberry Cheese Tart

TIP

To save time, use a store-bought pre-baked pastry shell.

•

For the smoothest filling, use extra smooth ricotta cheese.

PREHEAT OVEN TO 350° F (180° C)
8-INCH (20 CM) FLAN PAN WITH REMOVABLE BOTTOM

Crust

1 cup	all-purpose flour	250 ml
4 tsp	granulated sugar	20 mL
6 tbsp	cold margarine	90 mL
1/2 tsp	vanilla extract	2 mL
3 to 4 tsp	water	15 to 20 mL

Filling

1/2 cup	5% ricotta cheese	125 mL
1/2 cup	low-fat strawberry yogurt	125 mL
4 cups	fresh strawberries	1 L
1/4 cup	fruit jelly	50 mL
1 tbsp	water	15 mL

Icing sugar

PER SERVING

CALORIES	152
PROTEIN	3 G
FAT	7 G
CARBOHYDRATES	17 G
CHOLESTEROL	7 MG
SODIUM	140 MG

— *The Pointe* —
ARIZONA

1. Make the crust: Stir together flour and sugar. Cut in margarine until crumbly. Using a fork, toss in vanilla and enough water to make the dough come together. Press into pan. Chill 30 minutes. Bake 20 to 25 minutes or until golden. Cool on wire rack.

2. Make the filling: With an electric mixer, beat ricotta with yogurt until smooth. Spread over bottom of cooled crust. Cut stems off strawberries and place berries stem-side down on filling. In a small saucepan, melt fruit jelly with water; brush over strawberries.

3. Serve dusted with sifted icing sugar.

Fresh Fruit Tart

| 1 | 8-inch (20 cm) pastry shell, baked (see recipe, page 64) | 1 |

Filling

1 cup	skim milk	250 mL
2 tbsp	granulated sugar	25 mL
1 tsp	grated lemon zest	5 mL
1 tsp	grated orange zest	5 mL
1/2 tsp	vanilla extract	2 mL
1	egg, beaten	1
1 tbsp	cornstarch	15 mL
	Fresh berries and/or sliced fruit	
2 tbsp	redcurrant jelly	25 mL

1. Make the filling: In a saucepan heat milk over medium heat until hot. Stir in sugar, lemon zest, orange zest and vanilla. In a bowl, beat egg with cornstarch until blended. Whisk a little of the hot milk into egg mixture, then pour back into remaining milk. Whisk constantly until mixture is thick enough to coat a spoon; do not boil. Chill.

2. Spread custard over baked crust. Decorate with fruit and berries. In a saucepan, melt jelly. Brush over fruit.

Hot Blueberry Cobbler

PREHEAT OVEN TO 350° F (180° C)
8-INCH (2 L) SQUARE BAKING DISH

4 1/2 cups	blueberries	1.125 L
1/3 cup	water	75 mL
2 1/2 tbsp	granulated sugar	32 mL
1 tsp	grated lemon zest	5 mL
1/2 cup	whole-wheat flour	125 mL
1/2 cup	rolled oats	125 mL
1/4 cup	packed brown sugar	250 mL
1/4 cup	butter, softened	50 mL
1/4 tsp	cinnamon	1 mL
1/8 tsp	almond extract	0.5 mL

Honey Yogurt Topping (optional)

2 cups	low-fat yogurt	500 mL
	Honey to taste	

1. In a saucepan combine blueberries, water, sugar and lemon zest. Bring to a boil. Reduce heat and simmer for 2 minutes. Transfer to baking dish; set aside.

2. In a bowl, stir together whole-wheat flour, oats, brown sugar, butter, cinnamon and almond extract until crumbly. Sprinkle over blueberry mixture.

3. Bake for 30 minutes or until golden. Meanwhile, make the topping, if desired: In a bowl, stir together yogurt and honey until smooth.

4. Serve cobbler warm or at room temperature, topped with honey-yogurt, if desired.

Serves 6

PER SERVING

CALORIES	148
PROTEIN	2 G
FAT	7 G
CARBOHYDRATES	21 G
CHOLESTEROL	0 MG
SODIUM	38 MG

— *The Greenhouse* —
TEXAS

Crunchy Apple Cobbler

PREHEAT OVEN TO 375° F (190° C)
8-INCH (1.2 L) ROUND CAKE PAN

Filling

3	large apples	3
2 tbsp	lemon juice	25 mL
4 tsp	melted margarine	20 mL
2 tsp	honey	10 mL
3/4 tsp	cinnamon	4 mL

Topping

1/2 cup	all-purpose flour	125 mL
3 tbsp	granulated sugar *or* 2 tbsp (25 mL) fructose	45 mL
3/4 tsp	baking powder	4 mL
2 tbsp	margarine	25 mL
1 tbsp	raisins	15 mL
1 tbsp	2% milk	15 mL

1. Peel, core and quarter apples. In a bowl toss apples with lemon juice. Stir in margarine, honey and cinnamon. Transfer to cake pan. Bake for 10 minutes.

2. Meanwhile, make the topping: In a bowl, stir together flour, sugar and baking powder. Cut in margarine until crumbly. Stir in raisins and milk. Sprinkle over apples. Bake 15 minutes longer or until apples are tender and topping is golden.

3. Serve warm or at room temperature.

Serves 12

TIP

If you don't have a plastic squeeze bottle, put chocolate into a small plastic bag, then snip off the corner.

•

For a spider-web effect, draw chocolate lines in concentric circles over pie, then pull a toothpick across the lines.

PER SERVING

CALORIES	187
PROTEIN	5 G
FAT	8 G
CARBOHYDRATES	21 G
CHOLESTEROL	43 MG
SODIUM	182 MG

— Cal-A-Vie —
CALIFORNIA

Chocolate Swirl Pie

PREHEAT OVEN TO 350° F (180° C)
9-INCH (23 CM) PIE PLATE SPRAYED WITH BAKING SPRAY

Crust

1 1/2 cups	graham cracker crumbs	375 mL
3 tbsp	butter	45 mL
1 tbsp	brown sugar	15 mL
1/2 tsp	cinnamon	2 mL
1	egg white	1

Filling

3 oz	semi-sweet chocolate, chopped	75 g
12 oz	silken soft tofu	375 g
1/2 cup	low-fat yogurt	125 mL
1/4 cup	honey	50 mL
2	eggs	2
2 tsp	vanilla extract	10 mL
1/4 tsp	salt	1 mL

1. In a food processor, combine graham cracker crumbs, butter, brown sugar, cinnamon and egg white; process until crumbly. Pat onto bottom and sides of prepared pie plate. Set aside.

2. In a bowl set over hot (not boiling) water, melt chocolate, stirring until smooth; set aside. In a food processor, combine tofu, yogurt, honey, eggs, vanilla and salt; process until smooth. Pour into crust. Pour melted chocolate into a plastic squeeze bottle. Draw lines across pie at 1-inch (2.5 cm) intervals. Pull a toothpick across lines at regular intervals to create swirl pattern.

3. Bake for 30 minutes or until pie is loose just at center. Cool to room temperature on wire rack. Chill for at least 2 hours before serving.

Serves 6

TIP

For extra maple flavor, omit the vanilla and use 2 tsp (10 mL) maple extract.

PER SERVING

CALORIES	87
PROTEIN	4 G
FAT	3 G
CARBOHYDRATES	10 G
CHOLESTEROL	54 MG
SODIUM	65 MG

— The Heartland —
ILLINOIS

Maple Flan with Walnuts

PREHEAT OVEN TO 325° F (160° C)
4-CUP (1 L) SOUFFLÉ OR CASSEROLE DISH

2	egg whites	2
1	egg	1
2 1/2 tbsp	maple syrup	32 mL
1 tsp	vanilla extract	5 mL
1 tsp	maple extract	5 mL
1 1/2 cups	2% milk	375 mL

Toasted chopped nuts (optional)
CINNAMON CREAM (optional)
(see recipe, page 73)

1. In a bowl whisk together egg whites, whole egg, maple syrup, vanilla and maple extract until smooth. Gradually add milk, whisking constantly. Pour into soufflé dish.

2. Set dish in larger pan; pour in enough hot water to come halfway up sides. Bake for 60 minutes or until set. Remove from water bath; cool on wire rack. Chill.

3. Serve with toasted chopped nuts and/or cinnamon cream, if desired.

Pumpkin Flan

PREHEAT OVEN TO 325° F (160° C)
4-CUP (1 L) SOUFFLÉ OR CASSEROLE DISH

3/4 cup	canned pumpkin	175 mL
2 1/2 tbsp	fructose	32 mL
2	egg whites	2
1	egg	1
1/2 tsp	almond extract	2 mL
1/2 tsp	vanilla extract	2 mL
1/4 tsp	cinnamon	1 mL
1/8 tsp	ground cloves	0.5 mL
1 cup	2% milk	250 mL

Cinnamon Cream

1 cup	5% ricotta cheese	250 mL
4 tsp	maple syrup *or* honey	20 mL
3/4 tsp	cinnamon	4 mL

1. In a bowl, beat pumpkin, fructose, egg whites, whole egg, almond extract, vanilla extract, cinnamon and cloves until smooth. In a saucepan, heat milk until almost boiling; remove from heat. Whisk hot milk into pumpkin mixture. Pour into dish.

2. Set dish in larger pan; pour in enough hot water to come halfway up sides. Bake for 40 minutes or until set. Remove from water bath; cool on wire rack. Chill.

3. Make the cinnamon cream: In a food processor, purée ricotta, maple syrup and cinnamon until smooth. Serve with flan.

Serves 6

PER SERVING

CALORIES	114
PROTEIN	4 G
FAT	3 G
CARBOHYDRATES	20 G
CHOLESTEROL	54 MG
SODIUM	48 MG

— *Cal-a-Vie* —
CALIFORNIA

Butternut Squash Flan

PREHEAT OVEN TO 350° F (180° C)
SIX 1-CUP (250 mL) CUSTARD CUPS OR RAMEKINS

1 lb	butternut squash, peeled and cubed	500 g
1/4 cup	honey	50 mL
1/2 tsp	vanilla extract	2 mL
1/2 tsp	cinnamon	2 mL
1/4 tsp	ground cloves	1 mL
1/8 tsp	nutmeg	0.5 mL
1 1/4 cups	2% milk	300 mL
1	egg	1
1	egg white	1

1. In a pot of boiling water, cook squash until tender. Drain. In a food processor, purée squash until smooth. Add honey, vanilla, cinnamon, cloves and nutmeg; purée until well mixed. Transfer to a bowl; set aside.

2. In a saucepan heat milk over medium heat until bubbles appear at the edges. In a bowl whisk together whole egg, egg white and hot milk. Pour mixture through a strainer into squash mixture. Stir until well mixed. Divide mixture among custard cups.

3. Set custard cups in large pan; pour in enough hot water to come halfway up sides. Bake 45 minutes or until tester inserted in center comes out clean. Remove from water bath; cool on wire rack. Refrigerate leftovers.

Cookies & Breads

Zucchini Pineapple Bread

TIP

If you prefer carrot cake, substitute grated carrots for the zucchini.

PER SERVING	
CALORIES	103
PROTEIN	2 G
FAT	3 G
CARBOHYDRATES	16 G
CHOLESTEROL	18 MG
SODIUM	9 MG

— Canyon Ranch —
ARIZONA AND MASSACHUSETTS

PREHEAT OVEN TO 350° F (180° C)
9- BY 5-INCH (2 L) LOAF PAN SPRAYED WITH BAKING SPRAY

1 1/2 cups	whole-wheat flour	375 mL
1/2 cup	fructose	125 mL
1 tsp	baking powder	5 mL
1/2 tsp	baking soda	2 mL
1/4 tsp	cinnamon	1 mL
1/4 tsp	ground cloves	1 mL
1/4 tsp	ground nutmeg	1 mL
1 1/4 cups	packed grated zucchini	300 mL
1/2 cup	drained crushed pineapple	125 mL
3 tbsp	corn oil	45 mL
1	egg	1
1	egg white	1
1 tsp	vanilla extract	5 mL

1. In a large bowl, stir together flour, fructose, baking powder, baking soda, cinnamon, cloves and nutmeg. Set aside.

2. In another bowl, stir together zucchini, pineapple, corn oil, whole egg, egg white and vanilla. Stir into dry ingredients just until combined. Pour into prepared loaf pan.

3. Bake 45 to 55 minutes or until cake tester inserted in center comes out clean. Cool in pan 5 minutes. Remove from pan and cool on wire rack.

TIP

Use a pastry bag with a star tip and pipe the mixture onto baking sheet for an elegant cookie.

PER SERVING

CALORIES	34
PROTEIN	0.9 G
FAT	2 G
CARBOHYDRATES	3 G
CHOLESTEROL	0 MG
SODIUM	19 MG

— Sonoma Mission Inn and Spa —
CALIFORNIA

Vanilla Almond Snaps

PREHEAT OVEN TO 275° F (140° C)
BAKING SHEET LINED WITH PARCHMENT PAPER AND SPRAYED WITH BAKING SPRAY

3/4 cup	whole blanched almonds	175 mL
1/4 cup	granulated sugar	50 mL
1/4 tsp	salt	1 mL
2	egg whites	2
2 tbsp	granulated sugar	25 mL
1/2 tsp	vanilla extract	2 mL
	Sliced almonds (optional)	

1. In a food processor, grind almonds with 1/4 cup (50 mL) sugar and salt until as fine as possible. Transfer to a bowl and set aside.

2. In another bowl, beat egg whites until soft peaks form. Gradually add 2 tbsp (25 mL) sugar, beating until stiff peaks form. Fold in vanilla. Fold into ground nut mixture until blended. Drop by teaspoonfuls (5 mL) onto prepared baking sheet. If desired, sprinkle with a few sliced almonds.

3. Bake for 25 minutes or until golden.

Makes about 40

PER SERVING	
CALORIES	**83**
PROTEIN	**1** G
FAT	**5** G
CARBOHYDRATES	**9** G
CHOLESTEROL	**16** MG
SODIUM	**18** MG

— Turnberry Isle Yacht and Country Club —
FLORIDA

Raisin Honey Cookies

PREHEAT OVEN TO 350° F (180° C)
BAKING SHEET SPRAYED WITH BAKING SPRAY

1/2 cup	water	125 mL
1 cup	raisins	250 mL
1/2 cup	vegetable oil	125 mL
1/3 cup	honey	75 mL
2	medium eggs	2
1/2 tsp	vanilla extract	2 mL
1 1/2 cups	whole-wheat flour	375 mL
1/2 cup	chopped nuts	125 mL
1/4 cup	wheat germ	50 mL
1 tsp	cinnamon	5 mL
1/2 tsp	baking powder	2 mL
1/4 tsp	salt	1 mL
1/8 tsp	ground allspice	0.5 mL
1/8 tsp	ground cloves	0.5 mL
1/8 tsp	ground nutmeg	0.5 mL

1. In a small saucepan, bring water to a boil. Stir in raisins, reduce heat and simmer for 5 minutes. Drain. Cool.

2. In a bowl, beat together oil, honey, eggs and vanilla. Stir in raisins. In another bowl, stir together whole wheat flour, nuts, wheat germ, cinnamon, baking powder, salt, allspice, cloves and nutmeg. Stir into raisin mixture. Drop by teaspoonfuls (5 mL) onto prepared baking sheet.

3. Bake for 8 minutes or until golden.

Banana Walnut Bread

PREHEAT OVEN TO 375° F (190° C)
9- BY 5-INCH (2 L) LOAF PAN SPRAYED WITH BAKING SPRAY

2	ripe bananas, mashed	2
1/2 cup	butter, softened	125 mL
1/2 cup	granulated sugar	125 mL
1	egg	1
1	egg white	1
1 1/3 cups	whole-wheat flour	325 mL
1/3 cup	chopped walnuts	75 mL
1 tsp	baking soda	5 mL
1/4 tsp	salt	1 mL
1/4 cup	hot water	50 mL
	Sesame seeds *or* extra chopped walnuts (optional)	

1. In a bowl, beat bananas with butter until well mixed. Beat in sugar, whole egg and egg white until fluffy.

2. In another bowl, stir together flour, walnuts, baking soda and salt. Stir into banana mixture along with hot water just until blended. Pour into prepared loaf pan. If desired, sprinkle with sesame seeds or extra chopped walnuts.

3. Bake for 35 to 45 minutes or until cake tester inserted in center comes out clean. Cool in pan for 5 minutes. Remove from pan and cool on wire rack.

Makes about 45

Crisp Nut Cookies

PER SERVING	
CALORIES	63
PROTEIN	1 G
FAT	2 G
CHOLESTEROL	17 MG
CARBOHYDRATES	10 G
SODIUM	20 MG

— Sonoma Mission Inn —
and Spa
CALIFORNIA

PREHEAT OVEN TO 350° F (180° C)
BAKING SHEET SPRAYED WITH BAKING SPRAY

2	eggs	2
3/4 cup	granulated sugar	175 mL
6 tbsp	melted butter	90 mL
1/4 cup	water	50 mL
2 tsp	vanilla extract	10 mL
1 tsp	almond extract	5 mL
2 1/2 cups	all-purpose flour	625 mL
1/2 cup	chopped nuts	125 mL
2 1/4 tsp	baking powder	11 mL

1. In a bowl, beat eggs with sugar until well mixed. Beat in butter, water, vanilla and almond extract.

2. In another bowl, stir together flour, nuts and baking powder. Stir into egg-sugar mixture until dough forms a ball. Divide dough in half. Form each half into a log 12 inches (30 cm) long. Put on prepared baking sheet.

3. Bake for 20 minutes. Cool for 5 minutes. Cut on the diagonal into 1/2-inch (1 cm) thick slices. Bake for 20 minutes or until golden.

PER SERVING

CALORIES	49
PROTEIN	0.9 G
FAT	2 G
CARBOHYDRATES	6 G
CHOLESTEROL	10 MG
SODIUM	56 MG

— Norwich Inn and Spa —
CONNECTICUT

Oatmeal Raisin Cookies

PREHEAT OVEN TO 375° F (190° C)
BAKING SHEET SPRAYED WITH BAKING SPRAY

6 tbsp	packed brown sugar	90 mL
1/4 cup	butter, softened	50 mL
1	egg	1
1 tsp	vanilla extract	5 mL
1/2 cup	rolled oats	125 mL
1/2 cup	raisins	125 mL
1/4 cup	whole-wheat flour	50 mL
1/4 cup	wheat germ	50 mL
1/2 tsp	baking powder	2 mL

1. In a bowl cream brown sugar with butter. Beat in egg and vanilla. In another bowl, stir together oats, raisins, whole-wheat flour, wheat germ and baking powder. Stir into creamed mixture just until blended.

2. Drop batter by teaspoonfuls (5 mL) onto prepared baking sheet, leaving 2 inches (5 cm) between cookies. Bake for 10 to 12 minutes or until golden. Cool on wire racks.

Makes about 40

TIP

Use a natural, all-peanut type of peanut butter.

PER SERVING	
CALORIES	103
PROTEIN	2G
FAT	3G
CARBOHYDRATES	16 G
CHOLESTEROL	18 MG
SODIUM	9 MG

— Turnberry Isle Yacht and Country Club —
FLORIDA

Peanut Butter Cookies

PREHEAT OVEN TO 350° F (180° C)
BAKING SHEET SPRAYED WITH BAKING SPRAY

1/2 cup	peanut butter	125 mL
1/2 cup	packed brown sugar	125 mL
1/3 cup	margarine	75 mL
1	egg	1
1 tsp	vanilla extract	5 mL
1/2 cup	all-purpose flour	125 mL
2 tbsp	sesame seeds	25 mL
3/4 tsp	baking soda	4 mL
1/2 tsp	nutmeg	2 mL

Coating (optional)

1	egg white, beaten	1
1/2 cup	wheat germ	125 mL

1. In a bowl, beat peanut butter, brown sugar, margarine, egg and vanilla until light and fluffy. In another bowl, stir together flour, sesame seeds, baking soda and nutmeg. Stir flour mixture into peanut butter mixture just until combined. Form into 1-inch (2.5 cm) balls. If desired, dip balls in egg white, then roll in wheat germ. Put on prepared baking sheet.

2. Bake for 10 to 12 minutes or until golden.

Serves 16

TIP

For an extra calcium boost, try using part or all dried figs instead of dates.

PER SERVING	
CALORIES	83
PROTEIN	1 G
FAT	3 G
CARBOHYDRATES	13 G
CHOLESTEROL	0 MG
SODIUM	1 MG

— The Heartland —
ILLINOIS

Date Nut Bar

8-INCH SQUARE (2 L) BAKING DISH

1 1/3 cups	chopped dates	325 mL
1/4 cup	walnut pieces	50 mL
1/4 cup	whole almonds	50 mL
1/2 cup	granola	125 mL

1. In a food processor, combine dates, walnuts and almonds; process until mixture begins to come together.

2. Sprinkle half of granola over bottom of baking dish. Press date mixture firmly and evenly over granola. Top with remaining granola, pressing down slightly to embed in date mixture. Chill.

3. Cut into squares.

Peanut Butter Granola Rolls

TIP

Use a natural, all-peanut type of peanut butter.

Store-bought granola can be high in fat; be sure to buy a low-fat variety.

PER ROLL

CALORIES	52
PROTEIN	2 G
FAT	3 G
CARBOHYDRATES	4 G
CHOLESTEROL	0 MG
SODIUM	20 MG

The Heartland
ILLINOIS

3/4 cup	peanut butter	175 mL
1/4 cup	apple butter	50 mL
1/4 cup	raisins	50 mL
1 1/2 cups	granola	375 mL
1/4 cup	water	50 mL
2 tbsp	wheat germ	25 mL

1. In a food processor, blend peanut butter, apple butter and raisins until raisins are finely chopped. Alternately add granola and water, making three additions of granola and two of water, and processing until mixture comes together.

2. Roll each 1 tbsp (15 mL) of mixture into a ball. Roll balls in wheat germ.

About the Spas

CAL-A-VIE (CALIFORNIA). On 125 acres of wooded valley in North San Diego County, this exclusive spa was founded in 1986. In addition to fitness programs, massage and beauty treatments, it offers low-calorie gourmet meals, highlighted by herbs and vegetables from the spa's own garden.

CANYON RANCH (ARIZONA AND MASSACHUSETTS). Founded by real-estate magnate Mel Zuckerman in 1978, this spa offers programs geared to balancing mind, body and spirit. Recipes featured here were created by noted "Cook it Light" author Jeanne Jones.

DORAL SATURNIA (FLORIDA). Combining American-style fitness programs with classic European spa treatments, this exceptionally beautiful spa offers Italian cuisine with fat and calories reduced, but taste intact.

FOUR SEASONS RESORT AND CLUB (TEXAS). This large (315-suite) resort boasts unparalleled personal service and virtually every important health and beauty treatment imaginable. German-born executive chef Berhard Muller brings European flair to the kitchen, while keeping calories low.

GOLDEN DOOR (CALIFORNIA). Replicating the restorative care travelers receive at Japanese *honjin* inns, this 177-acre luxury resort pampers guests with low-fat creations from chef Tracy Pikhart Ritter. Meals are served with Japanese flair, balancing flavors and textures with nutrition.

THE GREENHOUSE (ARIZONA). Located midway between Dallas and Fort Worth, this luxury retreat offers a gentle health regime amidst gorgeous surroundings. Executive chef Michele Tezak presents sumptuous 850-calorie-a-day meals of natural fresh food.

GURNEY'S INN RESORT AND SPA (NEW YORK). Romantically located on a strip of sandy beach on the Atlantic Ocean, this spa offers a wide range of treatments, including unique seawater therapies. Cuisine is excellent, featuring high-fiber, low-fat creations with little salt or sugar. Desserts are superb.

THE HEARTLAND (ILLINOIS). Located 80 miles south of Chicago, this spa focuses on fitness, stress-management and weight-loss programs. The menu is low-fat vegetarian, with unusual entrees such as pizza.

JIMMY LESAGE'S NEW LIFE SPA (VERMONT). At the foot of the Stratton Mountains, guests lodge in two-storey Austrian-style chalets that provide a homey, informal atmosphere. Nutrition is a Lesage specialty. Delightful low-fat/high-fiber meals help trim inches painlessly.

KING RANCH HEALTH SPA AND FITNESS RESORT (ONTARIO, CANADA). Relaxed elegance and natural surroundings characterize this northern resort. Cuisine is healthy and appealing, with exciting desserts.

LA COSTA HOTEL AND SPA (CALIFORNIA). This massive (478-unit) but well-appointed spa lies 30 miles north of San Diego and is a favorite with celebrities and business executives alike. Low-fat gourmet meals are tasty, nourishing and beautifully served.

MAINE CHANCE (ARIZONA). Named for the Waterville, Maine summer home of founder Elizabeth Arden, this exclusive establishment offers the tasteful style of the quietly wealthy. Executive chef Harris Golden serves up light cuisine that is legendary, especially his desserts.

NORWICH INN AND SPA (CONNECTICUT). Blending historical New England ambiance with the feel of an English stately home, this spa offers an eclectic cuisine that includes locally grown produce and fresh seafood.

PALM AIRE (FLORIDA). Founded in 1971, this 1500-acre resort offers a mind-boggling range of facilities, including 37 tennis courts. Scrumptious desserts are the perfect reward for energy well expended.

THE POINTE (ARIZONA). With 1,840 suites and 10 restaurants, this resort is practically a city unto itself. Facilities and programs are too numerous to count. Meals range from casual to elegant, with wonderful light desserts.

RANCHO LA PUERTA (MEXICO). Located across the Mexican border, just 40 miles southeast of San Diego, this spa offers a natural desert landscape and a dry, gentle climate. Established over 50 years ago, it may be the birthplace of spa cuisine; meals are all-natural and low in cholesterol.

SAFETY HARBOR (FLORIDA). Built in 1926, this spa is located at the site of mineral springs first discovered in the 16th century by Spanish explorer Hernando de Soto. Cuisine is low in fat but packed with flavor.

SONOMA MISSION INN (CALIFORNIA). In the heart of Sonoma wine country near San Francisco, this lovely spa dates back to 1895, when hot water springs were discovered on the property. After a day of medicinal mud treatments, guests enjoy the inn's award-winning light cuisine.

THE SPA AT TOPNOTCH (VERMONT). As the name suggests, facilities at this four-star resort are excellent. Rated as one of America's top 10 restaurants, the resort prescribes a "diet for life" — one that is realistic, rewarding and takes into account age, activity level, lifestyle and favorite foods.

TURNBERRY ISLE YACHT AND COUNTRY CLUB (FLORIDA). Here's a spa that redefines exclusivity — it caters to just 10 guests at a time. Individual attention is extended to each guest, including a personalized menu developed in consultation with the spa's nutritionist.

Index

More of your favorite recipes

Just about everyone loves pasta. After all, there are few types of food that can be prepared in so many interesting ways. And that's what you'll discover in this book — over 50 recipes that range from classic comfort foods such as macaroni and cheese to more exotic Asian-inspired noodle dishes.

ISBN 1-896503-74-8

Robert Rose's
Favorite
PASTA

RECIPES SELECTED FROM BYRON AYANOGLU • JOHANNA BURKHARD
ANDREW CHASE • BILL JONES • ROSE REISMAN • STEPHEN WONG

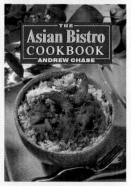